Kaleidoscope

Level C

Language Arts

SRA

Columbus, OH • Chicago, IL • Redmond, WA

The McGraw-Hill Companies

www.sra4kids.com

SRA

Send all inquiries to:
SRA/McGraw-Hill
8787 Orion Place
Columbus, OH 43240-4027

Printed in the United States of America.

ISBN 0-07-584231-9

4 5 6 7 8 9 QPD 07 06 05

The McGraw·Hill Companies

Table of Contents

UNIT 1

UNIT 2

Table of Contents

UNIT 3

UNIT 4

UNIT 5

Table of Contents

UNIT 6

Name ______________________________ Date ____________

Unit 1 • Grammar and Mechanics: Kinds of Sentences and End Punctuation

- A **statement** gives information. A statement ends with a **period (.).**
- An **imperative** gives a command. An imperative ends with a **period (.).**
- A **question** asks something. A question ends with a **question mark (?).**
- An **exclamation** expresses strong feelings. An exclamation ends with an **exclamation point (!).**

Identify each sentence as a question, an imperative, a statement, or an exclamation.

1. Ouch! That hurt! ____________________
2. I am going to the park on Saturday. ____________________
3. What are you doing tomorrow night? ____________________
4. Do your homework before you watch TV. ____________________
5. When will Sally be back in school? ____________________
6. Cal got a puppy for his birthday. ____________________

Write four sentences of your own. You should write one question, one imperative, one statement, and one exclamation.

7. ____

____

8. ____

____

9. ____

____

10. ____

____

Name ______________________________ Date ____________

Unit 1 • Vocabulary: Using a Dictionary

Review the following dictionary entry. In the lines that follow, identify the part of each numbered item. The first item has been completed for you.

fox \´fäks\ *noun* [ME, fr. OE; akin to OHG *fuhs* fox and perh. to Skt *puchha* tail] **1. a:** any of various carnivorous mammals of the dog family related to but smaller than wolves with shorter legs; more pointed muzzle; large erect ears; and long bushy tail **b:** the fur of a fox **2: a** clever crafty person

(1 = fox; 2 = \´fäks\; 3 = noun; 4 = [ME, fr. OE; akin to OHG fuhs fox and perh. to Skt puchha tail]; 5 = 1. a: any of various carnivorous mammals … long bushy tail; 6 = 2: a clever crafty person)

1. entry word
2. ____________________
3. ____________________
4. ____________________
5. ____________________
6. ____________________

Use a dictionary to answer the following questions.

7. What are the guide words for the entry *fox?* ____________________
8. How do you pronounce *fable?* ____________________
9. What is the first definition of the noun entry of *feast?* ____________________

____

10. What part of speech is the word *hunt* with the definition "to pursue for food or in sport"? ____________________

Name ______________________ Date __________

Unit 1 • Grammar and Mechanics: Complete and Incomplete Sentences

- A **complete sentence** has a **subject** and a **predicate.**
- An **incomplete sentence** is missing a **subject** or a **predicate.**
- The **subject** tells who or what the sentence is about.
- The **predicate** tells something about the subject.

Identify each of the following as complete or incomplete. If the sentence is incomplete, tell whether it is missing a subject or a predicate.

1. The girl in the red dress at the counter. ______________________
2. Ordered a large yogurt and celery sticks. ______________________
3. She dipped her celery sticks in the yogurt. ______________________
4. The yogurt was strawberry flavored. ______________________
5. On the way home the girl. ______________________

In the space provided, copy three sentences from your own writing and identify the subject and predicate of each.

6. ______________________

____

____

7. ______________________

____

____

8. ______________________

____

____

Name ______________________________ Date ______________

Unit 1 • Vocabulary: Homophones

Identify a homophone for each of the following words.

1. dew: ____________________
2. dye: ____________________
3. groan: ____________________
4. seem: ____________________
5. daze: ____________________

Underline the homophone that correctly completes each sentence.

6. The movie starts in an (hour / our).
7. I went to the county (fair / fare) with my family.
8. I got a (loan / lone) from my brother to buy my scooter.
9. I need a new (pair / pare / pear) of sneakers.
10. Which (way / weigh) to the park?

Name ______________________________ Date ______________

Unit 1 • Grammar and Mechanics: Identifying Subjects and Predicates

- The **subject** tells who or what the sentence is about.
- The **predicate** tells something about the subject.

Underline the subject once and the predicate twice for each of the following sentences.

1. The yellow flowers are blooming in my garden.
2. The chipmunk packed his cheeks full of nuts and seeds.
3. The Internet is a wonderful research tool.
4. Jennifer brought one of her paintings to school.
5. The man in the tweed suit is Uncle Karl.
6. My favorite fairy tale is "Little Red Riding Hood."
7. The cat and the dog play together for hours.
8. I can hardly wait to see our vacation pictures.
9. My family and I went to Puerto Rico last month.
10. Basketball is both fun and challenging.

Name ______________________________ Date ______________

Unit I • Vocabulary: Multiple-Meaning Words

For each word, write two possible definitions and use the word in a sentence.

1. **light**

definition 1: ______________________

definition 2: ______________________

sentence: ____

____

2. **pen**

definition 1: ______________________

definition 2: ______________________

sentence: ____

____

3. **right**

definition 1: ______________________

definition 2: ______________________

sentence: ____

____

Name ______________________ Date __________

Unit 1 • Grammar and Mechanics: General Review of Sentences

Identify each of the following sentences as complete or incomplete.

1. Why can't I go? ______________
2. The birds come to the birdfeeder every day. ______________
3. Can eat a whole pizza. ______________
4. (You) Be sure to lock the door. ______________
5. Watches television every night before bed. ______________

Now identify the subjects (underline once) and predicates (underline twice) of the complete sentences and note whether the incomplete sentences are missing a subject or predicate. Add a subject or predicate to the incomplete sentences.

In the space below, copy five sentences from your own writing. Identify whether they are complete or incomplete, the kinds of sentences they are, and their subjects (underline once) and predicates (underline twice).

6. ______________________________

____

7. ______________________________

____

8. ______________________________

____

9. ______________________________

____

10. ______________________________

____

Name ______________________________ Date ______________

Unit I • Vocabulary: Meaning from Context

Read the following sentences and write down what you think the underlined word means, based on the context clues in the sentence.

1. I was drenched by the rain because I forgot my umbrella and raincoat.

   word meaning: ______________________________

   ____

2. The verbose man talked, and talked, and talked. He would use one hundred words to say something that could be said with ten.

   word meaning: ______________________________

   ____

3. Jan gobbled the food so fast he didn't have time to taste it.

   word meaning: ______________________________

   ____

4. After losing the baseball game, I was sullen, refusing to talk to everybody, and disappointed.

   word meaning: ______________________________

   ____

5. Because today is July 13, the end of the fortnight will be July 27.

   word meaning: ______________________________

   ____

Name ______________________________ Date ______________

Unit 1 • Grammar and Mechanics: Common and Proper Nouns

- A **common noun** names **any** person, place, thing, or idea.
- A **proper noun** names a **particular** person, place, thing, or idea.

Read the following sentences and underline common nouns once and proper nouns twice.

1. When will Juan visit Puerto Rico next?
2. Margaret read *Bleak House* by Charles Dickens last July.
3. My favorite movie is James and the Giant Peach.
4. Alex and his family will go camping in Hocking Hills this summer.
5. Dana went to see a musical concert.

Fill in each blank with an appropriate proper noun.

6. My favorite book is ______________________________ ______________________________.
7. My favorite movie is ______________________________ ______________________________.
8. My favorite song is ______________________________ ______________________________.
9. If I could go to any city in the world, I would visit ______________ ______________________________.

Name ______________________________ Date ______________

Unit 1 • Vocabulary: Antonyms

Write an antonym for each of the listed words.

1. clean: ______________________
2. hot: ______________________
3. talkative: ______________________
4. asleep: ______________________
5. closed: ______________________
6. decrease: ______________________

Underline the antonyms in the following sentences.

7. I thought the movie was just beginning, but it was ending.
8. Kelly dropped the ball and then lifted it and tossed it to Danielle.
9. I was so hungry! When Dad served dinner, I ate too much, and then I was too full.
10. The enormous skyscraper towered over the minuscule church.

Name ______________________________ Date ____________

Unit I • Grammar and Mechanics: Irregular Plurals

Write the plural form of each word in the space provided.

1. goose: ____________________
2. deer: ____________________
3. ox: ____________________
4. child: ____________________
5. woman: ____________________
6. moose: ____________________

Write sentences using the correct plural forms for four of the words listed above.

7. ____

____

8. ____

____

9. ____

____

10. ____

____

Name ______________________ Date ____________

Unit 1 • Vocabulary: Synonyms

Write a synonym for each of the words below.

1. catch: ____________
2. power: ____________
3. false: ____________
4. laugh: ____________
5. smart: ____________
6. tired: ____________

Replace each underlined word with an appropriate synonym.

7. The captain <u>looked</u> out the porthole. ____________
8. It began to <u>rain</u> during the baseball game. ____________
9. I was <u>late</u> for school yesterday. ____________
10. The <u>scent</u> of the apple pie baking made me hungry.

____

Name ______________________________ Date ____________

Unit 2 • Grammar and Mechanics: Possessive Nouns

Write the correct possessive form of each of the following italicized words.

1. ____________________ textbook *(Kari)*
2. ____________________ office *(doctor)*
3. ____________________ nests *(birds)*
4. ____________________ votes *(people)*
5. ____________________ papers *(students)*

Write a sentence using each of the above possessives.

6. ____

____

7. ____

____

8. ____

____

9. ____

____

10. ____

____

Name ______________________________ Date ______________

Unit 2 • Vocabulary: Prefixes *dis-, re-, un-*

Add the appropriate prefixes (either *dis-*, *re-*, or *un-*) to the following words. Then write the definitions of the prefixed words.

1. loved: ______________________________
2. appear: ______________________________
3. tell: ______________________________
4. do: ______________________________
5. known: ______________________________
6. work: ______________________________

Write a paragraph using at least three words that include the prefixes taught in this lesson.

____

____

____

____

____

Name ______________________________ Date ____________

Unit 2 • Grammar and Mechanics: Review of Nouns

Underline the common nouns once and the proper nouns twice in the following sentences.

1. We went to the Grand Canyon for our summer vacation.
2. Kay and Sam went to the dance together.
3. Have you ever visited New York City?
4. My friends and I worked together on the project.
5. Tilly, my cat, sleeps on my feet every night.

Underline regular plurals once and the irregular plurals twice. Circle the possessive nouns.

6. The flock of geese flew south for the winter.
7. Jamal's parents were lawyers.
8. The deer lifted their heads as I approached.
9. My friend's dog loves to play fetch.
10. The people at the store were bargain hunting.

Name ________________________ Date ____________

Unit 2 • Vocabulary: Prefixes *pre-, in-, de-*

Fill in the missing spaces in the following chart.

Base/ Root Word	Prefix	Prefix Meaning	New Word
school	________	before	________
soak	pre-	________	presoak
sincere	________	not	________
fang	de-	________	defang
mature	________	before	________
complete	in-	________	________
frost	________	remove	________
determine	pre-	________	predetermine

Name ________________________________ Date ______________

Unit 2 • Grammar and Mechanics: Subject and Object Pronouns

Underline the pronoun that best completes each sentence.

1. (I / me) went to the store.
2. Janet gave (he / him) the key.
3. When will (we / us) get our report cards?
4. (She / her) baby-sits for (they / them).
5. Vinnie gave (I / me) a birthday present.
6. (They / them) were hoping for a sunny day.

Write a sentence using each of the listed pairs of pronouns.

7. (I / me) ____
8. (They / you) ____
9. (We / us) ____
10. (She / him) ____
11. (It / them) ____

Name ______________________ Date __________

Unit 2 • Vocabulary: Homophones

Underline the homophone that correctly completes each sentence.

1. (Their / There / They're) going to the football game tonight.
2. We burn (wood / would) in our fireplace.
3. I need to arrive (buy / by) six o'clock.
4. (Some / Sum) of us are going to the movies.
5. When will we (sea / see) you again?
6. Did you (hear / here) me?

Write homophones for the following words. Then use them in sentences.

7. hare: ______________________

____

8. eye: ______________________

____

9. wait: ______________________

____

10. sun: ______________________

____

Name ______________________________ Date ____________

Unit 2 • Grammar and Mechanics: Possessive Pronouns

Underline the pronoun that best completes each sentence.

1. Gina loaned me (her, hers) book.
2. (My, Mine) coat needs to be cleaned after the big rainstorm.
3. (Your, Yours) dog is in my yard.
4. Sarah and Alex came to (our, ours) play.
5. She walked (her, hers) dog to the park.

Write sentences using the following possessive pronouns properly.

6. his, her: ______________________________

____

7. their: ______________________________

____

8. my: ______________________________

____

9. its: ______________________________

____

10. your: ______________________________

____

Name ______________________________ Date ____________

Unit 2 • Vocabulary: Similes

In each of the following sentences, underline the simile and identify the topic. Then tell what the topic is compared to.

1. Dad grumbled like a bear when we woke him up at six in the morning.

   topic: ____________________ comparison: ____________________

2. When it came to math, she was like a human calculator.

   topic: ____________________ comparison: ____________________

3. After the race, Ben looked like a wilted flower.

   topic: ____________________ comparison: ____________________

4. Kim was as slow as a turtle when it was time to finish chores.

   topic: ____________________ comparison: ____________________

5. The boat bounced like a toy in the rough sea.

   topic: ____________________ comparison: ____________________

Write a sentence using each of the following as subjects of a simile.

6. school: ____

   ____

7. friends: ____

   ____

8. pets: ____

   ____

9. zoo: ____

   ____

10. clock: ____

    ____

Name ______________________________ Date ____________

Unit 2 • Grammar and Mechanics: Pronoun-Antecedent Agreement

For each item, circle the pronoun(s) and underline each antecedent.

1. The basketball doesn't bounce. It needs more air.
2. Sue ran toward the basket. She scored two points.
3. The crowd cheered for Sue. They loved her.
4. Coach Martin congratulated Sue. He said, "You have done well!"
5. Sue and her teammates won the game. They celebrated the victory.

Underline the pronoun that correctly completes each sentence.

6. My mom asked me to turn my radio down. (She / It) was too loud.
7. I called Mindy to ask (you / her) to come over to my house.
8. Andrew wrote a letter. He wants to mail (it / them) today.
9. The teachers had a meeting. (They / Them) discussed the school dance.
10. I broke my glasses. The eye doctor will fix (it / them).

Now write two sentence pairs of your own. In the second sentence, use a pronoun to replace a noun from the first sentence.

Example: The <u>pen</u> doesn't work. *It* is out of ink.

11. ____

____

12. ____

____

Name ______________________ Date ____________

Unit 2 • Vocabulary: Metaphors

For each item, underline the two things being compared.

1. Life is a journey filled with challenges.
2. Her room was a safe harbor where she could rest a while.
3. When it comes to keeping secrets, Juan is a lock with no key.
4. Freedom is an eagle flying high in the clouds.
5. Memory is a photo album filled with snapshots.

Write metaphors to compare each of the following words to something else.

6. friendship: ______________________

____

7. a seed: ______________________

____

8. autumn: ______________________

____

9. sunrise: ______________________

____

10. honesty: ______________________

____

Name ______________________________ Date ______________

Unit 2 • Grammar and Mechanics: Review of Pronouns

Underline the pronouns and circle any antecedents in each item below.

1. Kylie realized that she had lost her keys.
2. The family is very proud of their new house.
3. When Meena and Liz turned on the radio, they heard their favorite song.
4. Tyler noticed that his sister was walking behind him.
5. Liz's mother asked her, "Have you finished your homework?"

Underline the pronoun that correctly completes each sentence.

6. Tina's uncle sent (her / him) a birthday gift.
7. My teammates and (I / me) practice every day.
8. The neighbors enjoyed (our / their) vacation this year.
9. Jason loaned Tamara (his / her) sunglasses.
10. Sydney and (her / she) are tennis partners.

Name ______________________________ Date ______________

Unit 2 • Vocabulary: Idioms

Choose the appropriate idiom from the list to complete the meaning of each sentence.

down in the dumps	hold your horses	in hot water
pulling my leg	on its last leg	

1. When Jamie told me my favorite actor was outside, I knew she was ____________________.
2. Sammy hasn't smiled at all today. He must really be ____________________.
3. My computer is so old that it doesn't work well anymore. I think it is ____________________.
4. When my brother yelled at me to hurry, I said "____________________!"
5. My mother angrily called me by my full name, so I knew that I was ____________________.

Use the following idioms in sentences of your own.

6. hang in there: ____

____

7. the coast is clear: ____

____

8. hit the spot: ____

____

9. in a nutshell: ____

____

Name ______________________________ Date ____________

Unit 3 • Grammar and Mechanics: Regular Action Verbs

Underline the action verbs in the following sentences. Then identify whether they are present- or past-tense forms. For present-tense verbs, identify whether the subject is a singular or plural noun.

1. The young boy wanted his mother. ____________________
2. Janine works as an office manager. ____________________
3. Mindy and Andy live in Brooklyn. ____________________
4. Marta played the guitar very well. ____________________
5. The children visit the park every weekend. ____________________
6. The people in that house like flowers. ____________________

Fill in each of the following blanks with the proper form of the verb in the present tense.

7. Mrs. Callow often ____________________ chicken for dinner. *(cook)*
8. The Mitchell children ____________________ to school every day. *(walk)*
9. Danita and Hao ____________________ flowers in the spring. *(plant)*
10. Audience members ____________________ at the end of a performance. *(clap)*
11. The 43A bus ____________________ only on weekdays. *(run)*

Name ______________________________ Date ____________

Unit 3 • Vocabulary: Compound Words

Underline each compound word in the following sentences.

1. My grandmother will stay with us in May.
2. My baby-sitter lives downtown.
3. We will go waterskiing next weekend.
4. Don't forget your ice skates!
5. The sidewalk in front of our house needs repair.

Underline each of the compound words in the following sentences. Put a slash between the words that make up each compound.

6. I ate cottage cheese and pears for breakfast.
7. Be sure to wear your life jacket when you go waterskiing.
8. Many famous artists painted self-portraits.
9. She could not wait to try her surfboard in Hawaii.
10. Janet put on her raincoat and grabbed an umbrella on her way out the door.

Name ______________________________ Date ______________

Unit 3 • Grammar and Mechanics: Irregular Action Verbs

Insert the proper past-tense form of the irregular verbs.

1. Raymond ______________ the ball to Sandra. *(throw)*
2. Tara and Amelia ______________ across the field. *(run)*
3. Samantha ______________ her dog a new ball. *(buy)*
4. Renata was pleased when Ms. Delgado ______________ her for the school play. *(choose)*
5. Luis walked up the steps and ______________ the doorbell. *(ring)*

Write a sentence using the past-tense form of each of the following irregular verbs. If necessary, use a dictionary to identify the proper form.

6. see: ______________________________

____

7. write: ______________________________

____

8. fly: ______________________________

____

9. think: ______________________________

____

10. draw: ______________________________

____

Name ______________________________ Date ____________

Unit 3 • Vocabulary: Suffixes *-ful, -less, -ness*

Add an appropriate suffix to each of the following words. Then record the definition of the new word. Keep in mind that the spellings of the base words might change with the addition of the suffix.

1. hope: ______________________________
2. care: ______________________________
3. bright: ______________________________
4. motion: ______________________________
5. peace: ______________________________
6. color: ______________________________
7. good: ______________________________

Now write a brief paragraph using three of the preceding words with their suffixes.

____
____
____
____
____
____
____
____
____

Name ________________________________ Date ______________

Unit 3 • Grammar and Mechanics: Linking Verbs

Underline the linking verbs in the following sentences.

1. Pasta sounds good for dinner.
2. Janice is a point guard on the girls' basketball team.
3. Mom appears tired.
4. I became anxious as I read the scary book.
5. This dinner tastes great.
6. This blanket feels so soft and warm.

Write a sentence using each of the following verbs. Be sure to use the words as linking verbs, and not as action verbs or helping verbs.

7. seem: ____

____

8. be: ____

____

9. feel: ____

____

10. taste: ____

____

11. smell: ____

____

Name ______________________________ Date ______________

Unit 3 • Vocabulary: Suffixes *-ment, -tion/-sion, -phobia*

Fill in the missing spaces in the following chart.

Base/Root Word	Suffix	Suffix Meaning	New Word
success	-sion		
enjoy	-ment		
arachno-		fear or intolerance	
collide		act or process	collision
agora-	-phobia	fear or intolerance	
confine		state or condition	
claustro-	-phobia		
deplete	-tion	result of an act	
adjust	-ment		
confuse	-sion		

Name ______________________________ Date ______________

Unit 3 • Grammar and Mechanics: Verb Tenses

Underline each verb in the following sentences. Then identify the verb as past, present, or future tense.

1. I will travel to England this summer. ______________
2. Josephine watched my dogs for the weekend. ______________
3. David is my brother's name. ______________
4. We will eat vegetables and tofu for dinner. ______________
5. Liz walks a mile every day. ______________

Write three sentences for each of the following verbs. Use each verb in the past, the present, and the future tense. Check a dictionary if you are unsure of how to form the past tense of the irregular verb.

6. carry: ______________________________

____

____

7. stare: ______________________________

____

____

8. hold: ______________________________

____

____

Name ______________________________ Date ______________

Unit 3 • Vocabulary: Suffixes *-er, -ant, -ist*

Add one of the suffixes to each of the following words, and then use the word in a sentence of your own. You may consult a dictionary if necessary.

1. machine: ______________________________

____

2. work: ______________________________

____

3. account: ______________________________

____

4. walk: ______________________________

____

5. violin: ______________________________

____

6. real: ______________________________

____

7. play: ______________________________

____

8. attend: ______________________________

____

Name ______________________ Date ____________

Unit 3 • Grammar and Mechanics: Subject-Verb Agreement

Underline the subject once. Underline the verb twice. Write whether the verb is *singular* or *plural* on the line.

1. My house is near a large bridge. ____________
2. Bridges are an important part of New York City.

   ____

3. Many people ride bikes across the Brooklyn Bridge.

   ____

4. People walk across the bridge in the summer.

   ____

5. Jesse drives across the bridge to work every day.

   ____

Finish each sentence with a verb in the present tense. Make sure your verb agrees with the subject.

Example: The ducks ______________________.

6. Our new puppy ______________________.
7. The baseball players ______________________.

Underline the correct verb to complete each sentence.

8. Jesse (read / reads) one book each week.
9. The squirrels (play / plays) in the park.
10. Students (complete / completes) their homework on time.
11. Some animals (make / makes) great pets.
12. I (ride / rides) my bike every day.

Name ______________________________ Date ______________

Unit 3 • Vocabulary: Word Meanings from Context

Read each sentence below. Write a definition for the underlined word. Use context clues to help you.

1. The construction company wanted to demolish the old building, but many citizens wanted it to remain standing.

   Definition: ______________________________

   ____

2. The work of art was in the shape of a sphere, and it looked like a painted basketball.

   Definition: ______________________________

   ____

3. Shoppers can be divided into two groups: those who plan their purchases in advance, and impulse buyers.

   Definition: ______________________________

   ____

For each of the words below, write a sentence that uses context clues to help readers understand the meaning of the word. Feel free to use a dictionary or thesaurus to help you.

4. tadpoles: ______________________________

   ____

5. cleverly: ______________________________

   ____

6. forlorn: ______________________________

   ____

Name ______________________________ Date ______________

Unit 3 • Grammar and Mechanics: Review of Verbs

Underline the verb in each sentence. Write *action* or *linking* to tell what kind of verb it is.

1. Basketball is my favorite sport. ____________________
2. The team practices after school. ____________________
3. I play point guard for the team. ____________________

For the following sentences, write on the blank the correct past-tense form of the verb in parentheses.

4. Sydney ____________________ her guitar yesterday. *(sell)*
5. Her best friend ____________________ it from her. *(buy)*
6. Sydney ____________________ her friend how to play a song. *(teach)*

Underline the correct verb to complete each sentence.

7. Last summer, I (swimmed / swam) in my uncle's pool.
8. Taylor (exercise / exercises) every morning before school.
9. Some people (travel / traveled) many miles to see the concert last night.
10. The foghorn (was / were) one of many helpful inventions.
11. My father (teached / taught) me how to ride a bike.

Name ______________________________ Date ______________

Unit 3 • Vocabulary: Roots *claim, photo, struct*

For each item below, identify the root, and then write a definition of the word that uses the root's meaning. You may use a dictionary if you need help.

Example: structure ______________________________

1. reclaim: ______________________________

____

2. photocopy: ______________________________

____

3. instruct: ______________________________

____

4. exclaim: ______________________________

____

5. destruction: ______________________________

____

For each of the roots below, choose a word that includes the root, and then use the word in a sentence.

6. claim: ______________________________

____

7. photo: ______________________________

____

8. struct: ______________________________

____

Name ______________________________ Date ____________

Unit 4 • Grammar and Mechanics: Comparative and Superlative Adjectives

Underline each adjective, and draw an arrow to the word or words it modifies.

1. The gray cat and black dog slept in the bed.
2. Six people tried out for the basketball team.
3. Poppy was tired and thirsty after mowing the lawn.
4. Gina ate several pieces of candy after our early dinner.
5. The best place to get pizza is on my street.

Underline each comparative adjective once and each superlative adjective twice.

6. Scamp is the friendliest dog I ever met.
7. The most beautiful picture won the blue ribbon.
8. Cassie is younger than Joe.
9. This end of the pool is deeper than that end.
10. Planting trees is harder than planting flowers.

Name ______________________________ Date ______________

Unit 4 • Vocabulary: Roots *graph, junct*

Underline the root of each of the following words. Explain how its meaning relates to the meaning of the whole word. If necessary, use a dictionary to identify the meaning of the listed word.

1. autograph: ______________________________
2. paragraph: ______________________________
3. biography: ______________________________
4. graphite: ______________________________
5. conjunction: ______________________________
6. juncture: ______________________________
7. junction: ______________________________
8. adjunct: ______________________________

Name ______________________________ Date ______________

Unit 4 • Spelling: Roots *graph, junct*

For each of the following word pairs, circle the correctly spelled word and copy it in the space provided.

1. graphec

   graphic ______________________

2. phonograf

   phonograph ______________________

3. paragraph

   parigraph ______________________

4. junture

   juncture ______________________

5. conjunction

   conjuhntion ______________________

6. junkshun

   junction ______________________

Name ______________________________ Date ____________

Unit 4 • Grammar and Mechanics: Adverbs

Underline each adverb in the following sentences. Then tell whether it identifies *how, when, where,* or *to what degree.*

1. Yesterday, Kyle won the spelling championship.

   ____

2. Alan ate lunch quickly. ____________________
3. Janice is very tidy. ____________________
4. We played ball outside. ____________________
5. He will return to school tomorrow. ____________________

Underline each adverb once and the word it modifies twice.

6. The car sped quickly by our house.
7. I watched an extremely interesting documentary on television.
8. Kristi arrived late to the party.
9. Max worked enthusiastically on his report.
10. The bicyclist carefully crossed the busy intersection.

Name ______________________ Date __________

Unit 4 • Vocabulary: Word Meanings from Context

Use the context clues in the sentences below to determine the meanings of the underlined words.

1. The student's work was <u>adequate</u>. He could have done better, but it was not a bad job.

   Definition: ______________________

   ____

2. Unlike his troublesome stablemate, Daisy was a <u>docile</u> horse.

   Definition: ______________________

   ____

3. The new owner <u>refurbished</u> the house. She installed central air conditioning, replaced windows, and bought new appliances.

   Definition: ______________________

   ____

4. The dangerous driver was <u>oblivious</u> to traffic laws. This made him a danger to everyone on the road.

   Definition: ______________________

   ____

5. Computers <u>depreciate</u> quickly, and in a very few years they are worth almost nothing at all.

   Definition: ______________________

   ____

Name ______________________________ Date ____________

Unit 4 • Spelling: Sound/Spelling Review

Read the first word in each set. Then fill in the blanks to form a word that rhymes with the first word.

1. word b__________d
2. barber harb__________
3. sea kn__________
4. county bount__________
5. soil t__________
6. placid a__________d

Circle the correct spelling in each pair. Copy the word on the space provided.

7. advisir
   advisor ____________________
8. neat
   neet ____________________
9. anoint
   anoynt ____________________
10. cival
    civil ____________________
11. bee
    bea ____________________
12. rainee
    rainy ____________________

Name ______________________________ Date ____________

Unit 4 • Grammar and Mechanics: Review of Adjectives and Adverbs

Underline the adjectives in the following sentences.

1. Laptop computers are portable.
2. I want an orange kitten for my birthday.
3. The largest house on our block is being sold.
4. David's blue bike is new.
5. Tina wore a beautiful dress to the class dance.

Underline the adverbs in the following sentences.

6. "Help!" Carmen screamed loudly.
7. We decided against buying those shoes because of their extremely high price.
8. Cara silently agreed with the rest of the class.
9. Wendy laughed uncontrollably when she heard the joke.
10. Yesterday, we went to the mall.

Name ______________________ Date ____________

Unit 4 • Vocabulary: Idioms

Use the following idioms in sentences of your own.

1. have all your eggs in one basket: ______________________

____

2. stick your foot in your mouth: ______________________

____

3. cut and dried: ______________________

____

4. on cloud nine: ______________________

____

5. catch as catch can: ______________________

____

Name ______________________ Date __________

Unit 4 • Spelling: Frequently Misspelled Words

Write the word in parentheses that correctly completes each sentence.

1. His (close, clothes) were wrinkled. ______________
2. Nathan hoped to (receive, recieve) an invitation to the party. ______________
3. My gym teacher told me to remember to (breath, breathe) when I exercise. ______________
4. Kari (knew, new) that she did well on the test. ______________
5. Celia (rote, wrote) a letter to her pen pal last night. ______________
6. Jim was better at (cience, science) than he was at English. ______________
7. My mom said, "I (supose, suppose) you can go." ______________
8. Carol (knows, nows) Gina very well. ______________

Name ______________________ Date ____________

Unit 4 • Grammar and Mechanics: Conjunctions and Compound Sentences

Combine each of the following sets of simple sentences to make a compound sentence. Use a comma and the words *and, but,* or *or* to connect the sentences.

1. Kevin did his homework. Then he played outside. ______________________

____

2. The cat liked tuna. She did not like chicken. ______________________

____

3. Will you go to the mall? Will you go to the movies? ______________________

____

4. Lynn wanted to learn sign language. She also wanted to learn French.

____

____

5. Jack liked football. He disliked baseball. ______________________

____

Name ______________________________ Date ____________

Unit 4 • Vocabulary: Metaphor and Simile

In the space provided, identify whether each sentence contains a metaphor or a simile.

1. Joe's laughter was music to my ears. ____________

2. Laura raced around the track like a gazelle. ____________

3. Your smile was a beacon of light across the crowded room.

   ____

4. Karen stomped through the house like an elephant.

   ____

5. The people were packed in the elevator like sardines.

   ____

Use each of the following as subjects of a metaphor or a simile. Be sure to write at least one of each.

6. kindness: ______________________________

   ____

7. computer: ______________________________

   ____

8. competition: ______________________________

   ____

9. pizza: ______________________________

   ____

10. picture: ______________________________

    ____

Name ______________________ Date __________

Unit 4 • Spelling: Multisyllabic Words

Read aloud each of the following words, clapping the syllables as you read. Then record the number of syllables in the spaces provided.

1. spitefully: __________
2. idea: __________
3. myself: __________
4. entertaining: __________
5. flexibility: __________
6. musical: __________
7. unfortunately: __________
8. wager: __________

Name ______________________________ Date ______________

Unit 4 • Grammar and Mechanics: Prepositions and Prepositional Phrases

Underline the prepositional phrases in the following sentences.

1. I walked over the bridge across the river.
2. Kelly drank from that cup.
3. The baby ate its dinner with a spoon.
4. The boys go to bed after supper.
5. Jake has been sick since last week.
6. The apples on that tree are ripe.
7. We learned about George Washington in our history class.

Write sentences using the following prepositions to begin prepositional phrases.

8. in spite of: ______________________________

____

9. toward: ______________________________

____

10. without: ______________________________

____

Name ______________________ Date __________

Unit 4 • Vocabulary: Prefixes *micro-* and *ultra-*

Fill in each blank with the appropriate prefix.

1. The manager was ______________sensitive to the needs of his customers.
2. The announcer spoke into the ______________phone.
3. Janice heated up her lunch in the ______________wave oven.
4. Certain rays from the sun, called ______________violet rays, cause sunburns.
5. We used a ______________scope to look at the small life-forms in the water.
6. Because Ken took care of every specific detail, he was

   considered a ______________manager.
7. The ______________heat of the sun prohibits a rocket from landing there.
8. My mom told me to be ______________careful when I went rock climbing.

Name ______________________________ Date ____________

Unit 4 • Spelling: Prefixes *micro-* and *ultra-*

Using each word in the box once, fill in the blanks with the proper word.

microscope	ultrarealistic	ultrasonic
microorganisms	microfilm	ultraconvenient

1. In science class, we looked at single-celled organisms with a ____________________.
2. The jet plane traveled at ____________________ speeds.
3. The ____________________ painting made me feel as if I were surrounded by trees.
4. The library kept years of periodicals on ____________________.
5. Bacteria and plankton are examples of ____________________.
6. Having the grocery store around the corner is ____________________.

Name ______________________________ Date ______________

Unit 4 • Grammar and Mechanics: Review Parts of Speech

In the following sentences, underline the nouns once and the verbs twice.

1. Nancy was late for the meeting.
2. Gail and John played a game.
3. The dog slept at the foot of the bed.

In the following sentences, underline the adjectives once and the adverbs twice.

4. The old clock above my new desk ticked noisily.
5. Soon I will leave for a long vacation.
6. James was very excited about his new book.

In the following sentences, underline the pronouns once and the prepositions twice.

7. Her cat slept on my lap.
8. They wanted me at the counter.
9. I am late for school.

In the following sentences, underline the conjunctions once and the interjections twice.

10. Oh, well. I guess Jimmy and Sue are not coming.
11. Yikes! Look out for that snake and that tarantula!
12. Oh, no! I missed my bus, but I can walk to school.

Name ______________________________ Date ______________

Unit 4 • Vocabulary: Roots *tele* and *libre*

For each item below, identify the root, and then write a definition of the word that uses the root's meaning. You may use a dictionary if you need help.

Example: telephone tele—a device to make sounds travel across a distance

1. liberty: ______________________________

____

2. liberate: ______________________________

____

3. television: ______________________________

____

4. telescope: ______________________________

____

5. telegraph: ______________________________

____

For each of the roots below, choose a word that includes the root, and then use the word in a sentence.

6. tele: ______________________________

____

7. libre: ______________________________

____

Name ______________________________ Date ______________

Unit 4 • Spelling: Roots *tele* and *libre*

Choose a word from the box to fill in the blanks. Use each word in the box once.

liberally	telephone	liberty
telescope	Liberia	television

1. Jenna sprinkled salt ______________________ on her mashed potatoes.
2. While Kara was in Paris, I talked to her on the ______________________.
3. The founders of a new country named it ______________________ to celebrate their freedom.
4. We used a ______________________ to look at the stars.
5. ______________________ allows people to see and hear events happening half a world away.
6. The Statue of ______________________ is a symbol that the United States is a land of freedom.

Name ______________________________ Date ____________

Unit 5 • Grammar and Mechanics: Commas in a Series

Insert commas where necessary in the following sentences.

1. I have a rottweiler a black lab and three cats.
2. Do you your sister or your brother have any pets?
3. My dogs are big fast and clever.
4. My cats sleep on the chair under the table or in the bed.
5. My cat crept across the living room ran up the stairs and jumped into bed.

Write four sentences that require commas in a series. Follow the directions for each item.

6. Include four nouns. ______________________________

____

7. Include three adjectives. ______________________________

____

8. Include three verbs. ______________________________

____

9. Include three phrases. ______________________________

____

Name ______________________ Date ____________

Unit 5 • Vocabulary: Prefixes *il-, mis-, auto-*

Fill in the missing spaces in the following chart.

Base/ Root Word	Prefix	Prefix Meaning	New Word
pilot	________	self	________
communicate	________	wrongly, badly	________
logical	________	not	________
graph	________	self	________
quote	________	wrongly	________
legible	________	not	________
inform	________	wrongly	________
biography	________	self	________

Name ______________________________ Date ______________

Unit 5 • Spelling: Prefixes *il-, mis-, auto-*

Underline the correctly spelled word in each item. Then write each word on the space provided.

1. mispell

   misspell ______________

2. misstype

   mistype ______________

3. missmanage

   mismanage ______________

4. ilogical

   illogical ______________

5. illegible

   ilegible ______________

6. autobiography

   auttobiography ______________

7. auto-motive

   automotive ______________

8. auto-pilot

   autopilot ______________

Name ______________________________ Date ____________

Unit 5 • Grammar and Mechanics: Commas in Direct Address

Place commas where necessary in the following sentences. Not all sentences will contain direct address.

1. Please come in Dr. Fleming.
2. When will Ginni arrive?
3. Sadie I told you to sit and stay.
4. Janice told Keith about the party.
5. I think Coach Johnson that we will definitely win.

Use direct address in five sentences of your own.

6. ____

   ____

7. ____

   ____

8. ____

   ____

9. ____

   ____

10. ____

    ____

Name ______________________________ Date ____________

Unit 5 • Vocabulary: Prefixes *anti-, pro-, mal-;* Root Word *bene*

Define each of the following words, explaining how the root or prefix applies to the meaning. Use a dictionary if necessary.

1. antidote: ______________________________

2. malodor: ______________________________

3. malady: ______________________________

4. benefit: ______________________________

5. promote: ______________________________

6. progression: ______________________________

7. benediction: ______________________________

8. antislavery: ______________________________

Name ______________________________ Date ____________

Unit 5 • Spelling: Prefixes *anti-, pro-, mal-;* Root Word *bene*

Combine the following to make a word. Write each word on the space provided.

1. anti + venom = ____________________
2. anti + intrusion = ____________________
3. pro + tect = ____________________
4. pro + French = ____________________
5. mal + absorption = ____________________
6. mal + adapted = ____________________
7. bene + ficial = ____________________
8. bene + fit = ____________________

Name ______________________ Date __________

Unit 5 • Grammar and Mechanics: Punctuating Dialogue

Add the correct punctuation to the dialogue.

Yesterday explained Stu was my little brothers birthday

How old is he asked Kara

Stu replied He is four years old I can remember when my mom and dad brought him home the first time He was so small

Ill bet he isnt small anymore said Kara

Continue the conversation, making up dialogue for Kara and Stu. Use at least five sentences of dialogue. Be sure to punctuate it correctly and begin a new paragraph each time the speaker changes.

Name ______________________________ Date ____________

Unit 5 • Vocabulary: Suffixes *-able, -ible, -or*

Write the definition of each of the following words. Then use each word in a sentence. Use a dictionary if necessary.

1. editor: ______________________________
2. credible: ______________________________
3. counselor: ______________________________
4. edible: ______________________________
5. laughable: ______________________________
6. earnable: ______________________________

Name ______________________ Date ____________

Unit 5 • Spelling: Suffixes *-able, -ible, -or*

Fill in each blank with the correct spelling of each word with its suffix.

1. dissect + ible = ____________
2. manage + able = ____________
3. invest + or = ____________
4. adjust + able = ____________
5. jury + or = ____________

Circle the correctly spelled word in each set and copy it in the space provided.

6. adviseor
   advisor ____________
7. removeable
   removable ____________
8. reliable
   relyable ____________
9. dissectible
   dissecttible ____________
10. servicable
    serviceable ____________

Name ______________________________ Date ____________

Unit 5 • Grammar and Mechanics: Commas in a Series

Insert commas where necessary in the following sentences.

1. I will take a hamburger a milkshake and French fries.
2. Todd Jared and Tony went on a bike ride.
3. We drove down the street across the bridge and past the store.
4. Please bring a pen a pencil and blank paper with you to class.
5. The triathlon required participants to run bike and swim.

Write three sentences about the selection using commas in a series in each.

6. ______________________________

____

____

7. ______________________________

____

____

8. ______________________________

____

____

Name ______________________________ Date __________

Unit 5 • Vocabulary: Suffixes *-ly, -ment, -ery*

Follow the directions for each item below.

1. Change *late* to an adverb and use it in a sentence. ______________________________

____

____

2. Change *arrange* to a noun and use it in a sentence. ______________________________

____

____

3. Change *bake* to a noun and use it in a sentence. ______________________________

____

____

4. Change *near* to an adverb and use it in a sentence. ______________________________

____

____

5. Change *abandon* to a noun and use it in a sentence. ______________________________

____

____

Name ______________________________ Date ______________

Unit 5 • Spelling: Suffixes *-ly, -ment, -ery*

In the space provided, correct the spelling of each of the following words.

1. arguement: ______________________________
2. basment: ______________________________
3. entrappment: ______________________________
4. bakeery: ______________________________
5. nurserey: ______________________________
6. desperatly: ______________________________
7. sincereley: ______________________________
8. louddly: ______________________________

Name ______________________________ Date ____________

Unit 5 • Grammar and Mechanics: Punctuating Dialogue

Add quotation marks, commas, and end punctuation to the following sentences.

1. When will you start school asked Alicia
2. Karen replied I will start school in September When will you start
3. You have a longer break than I do said Alicia I will start at the end of August
4. Did Alicia say I will start at the end of August
5. Yes she did replied Jason
6. This summer exclaimed Kurt will be so much fun
7. I am looking forward to going to the beach the most said Jason
8. Kurt replied Having picnics is my favorite summer activity

Name ______________________ Date __________

Unit 5 • Vocabulary: Multiple-Meaning Words

Write two sentences for each of the following words. Use a different meaning in each sentence. If necessary, use a dictionary to determine the meanings of the words.

1. plants: ______________________

2. spoke: ______________________

3. stamp: ______________________

4. might: ______________________

5. saw: ______________________

Name ______________________________ Date ____________

Unit 5 • Spelling: Sound/Spelling Review

Read the first word in each set. Then fill in the blanks to form a word that rhymes with the first word.

1. latch ma________
2. deceive rel________ve
3. tacks fa________
4. bargain ________argon
5. switch whi________

Underline the correct spelling in each pair. Copy the word on the space provided.

6. engine
   enjine ____________________
7. original
   orijinal ____________________
8. wach
   watch ____________________
9. akse
   axe ____________________
10. chief
    cheif ____________________

Name ______________________________ Date ______________

Unit 5 • Grammar and Mechanics: Review of Sentences and Punctuation

Add the appropriate punctuation to the following passage.

Mrs Andrusco do you need any help asked Mitch You can take the little box the plastic bag and the book bag and I can take the suitcase

Thank you Mitchell replied Mrs Andrusco but I think Ill leave the suitcase for Mr Andrusco to carry There are some smaller bags inside Could I ask you to carry those instead

Wow exclaimed Mitch That sure is a lot of stuff for a weekend trip

Name ______________________ Date ____________

Unit 5 • Vocabulary: Idioms

Use the following idioms in sentences of your own.

1. let the cat out of the bag: ______________________________

____

____

2. a long shot: ______________________________

____

____

3. catch forty winks: ______________________________

____

____

4. under the weather: ______________________________

____

____

5. up a tree: ______________________________

____

____

Name ______________________________ Date ______________

Unit 5 • Spelling: Sound/Spelling Review

For each set of words, follow the specific directions. Use the pronunciation key at the beginning of the glossary to help you answer the questions.

1. Copy the words that make the /o͞o/ sound:

   foot, look, boot ______________________

   duty, music, human ______________________

   use, mute, flute ______________________

2. Copy the words that include the schwa sound:

   adore, redo ______________________

   thankful, observe ______________________

   income, hoping ______________________

Use the following spellings to complete the words listed below.

oo ue u_e u ng ea sh

3. J__________n__________

4. j__________nior

5. untr__________

6. impr__________dent

7. inst__________d

8. fli__________

9. t__________lbox

10. ch__________se

Name ______________________________ Date ____________

Unit 6 • Grammar and Mechanics: Review: Identifying Subjects and Predicates

In each of the following sentences, underline each simple subject once and each simple predicate twice.

1. Jennifer laughed and danced a little victory dance.
2. Two young girls enjoyed the puppet show.
3. They turned their backs and walked away.
4. He put the new cap on his head.
5. They approached the cave with caution.

Now put a line between the complete subject and complete predicate in each of the sentences above.

Name ______________________ Date __________

Unit 6 • Vocabulary: Roots *form, nov, rupt, bio*

Fill in each blank with a word from the box. Use each word once.

formation	biography	novel	disrupted
biologist	erupted	deformed	renovation

1. The volcano ______________ and lava spewed forth.
2. Inventors are always looking for ______________ ideas.
3. A ______________ is the story of someone's life.
4. The band marched down the field in ______________.
5. The knock at the door ______________ the writer's concentration.
6. Someone who studies the science of living things is called a ______________.
7. Their house looks so much better after the ______________.
8. The trees were stunted and ______________ due to the constant high winds.

Name ______________________________ Date ____________

Unit 6 • Spelling: Roots *form, nov, rupt, bio*

Combine the prefixes, roots, and suffixes below to make five words.

Roots	Prefixes	Suffixes
form	dis-	-tion
nov	trans-	-ate
rupt	in-	-ic
bio	e-	
	anti-	

1. ______________________
2. ______________________
3. ______________________
4. ______________________
5. ______________________

Circle the correctly spelled word and copy it on the space provided.

1. erupt
   errupt ______________________
2. formation
   formtion ______________________
3. novela
   novella ______________________
4. disrupt
   dissrupt ______________________
5. biography
   biotgraphy ______________________

Name ______________________ Date __________

Unit 6 • Grammar and Mechanics: Review of Verb Tenses

Underline each verb and identify it as *past, present,* or *future.*

1. The sunset was beautiful last night. ______________
2. I will visit my grandparents next summer. ______________
3. Basketball is my favorite sport. ______________
4. Jennifer wants a new bicycle. ______________
5. I will eat ice cream for dessert. ______________
6. Liz won the blue ribbon. ______________
7. Komal wrote a letter to Li. ______________
8. Emma goes to the park every Saturday. ______________
9. Kirsten and Tyler will play soccer next year. ______________
10. Sharon helped Julie with the box. ______________

Name ______________________________ Date ______________

Unit 6 • Vocabulary: Prefixes *bi-, tri-, dec-, multi-, poly-*

Write the definition of each of the following words.
Explain how the prefix relates to the meaning.
If necessary, consult a dictionary.

1. biped: ______________________________

____

____

2. trident: ______________________________

____

____

3. decathlon: ______________________________

____

____

4. multigrain: ______________________________

____

____

5. polyclinic: ______________________________

____

____

Name ______________________ Date ____________

Unit 6 • Spelling: Prefixes *bi-, tri-, dec-, multi-, poly-*

Combine the prefixes, roots, and suffixes below to make five words. If necessary, consult a dictionary.

Roots	**Prefixes**	**Suffixes**
angle	bi-	-al
culture	tri-	
cycle	dec- (or deca-)	
glot	multi-	
gon	poly-	

1. ______________________

2. ______________________

3. ______________________

4. ______________________

5. ______________________

Name ______________________________ Date ______________

Unit 6 • Grammar and Mechanics: Review of Regular and Irregular Plural Nouns

In the following paragraph, underline the regular plural nouns once and the irregular plural nouns twice. You will underline ten words.

Sequoya created a new alphabet for his people. The alphabet had 86 symbols—a symbol for every sound in the Cherokee language. The Cherokee men, women, and children learned the alphabet quickly. Soon after, they published books and newspapers using the new alphabet. This amazing invention changed the Cherokee people forever and made it possible to record their stories. Sequoya became one of the Cherokee heroes.

Name ______________________________ Date ____________

Unit 6 • Vocabulary: Word Families *read, real*

Explain how each set of words is related in meaning. You may use a dictionary if necessary.

1. reader. rereading, misread: ______________________________

____

____

____

____

____

2. reality, ultrarealistic, unreal: ______________________________

____

____

____

____

____

Name ______________________ Date __________

Unit 6 • Spelling: Sound/Spelling Review

Read the first word in each set. Then fill in the blanks in the second word to form a rhyme for the first word.

1. great m__________
2. deceive __________eceive
3. trap __________ap
4. very __________erry
5. look b__________k

Underline the correct spelling in each pair. Copy the word on the space provided.

1. graf

   graph ____________________
2. rong

   wrong ____________________
3. grat

   grate ____________________
4. foot

   phoot ____________________
5. wich

   which ____________________

Name ______________________________ Date ____________

Unit 6 • Grammar and Mechanics: Review of Subject-Verb Agreement

Identify the subject-verb agreement in the following sentences as *correct* or *incorrect*. If the sentence is incorrect, cross out the verb and write the correct verb in the space provided.

1. Dan and Lisa goes to that school. ____________________
2. I like ice cream and candy. ____________________
3. Either Columbus or Cleveland are their home. ____________________
4. Tilly wants a treat. ____________________
5. Vitamin C help your immune system. ____________________
6. Dani play basketball every night. ____________________
7. Spring and summer are my favorite seasons. ____________________
8. Either Mrs. George or her husband plant flowers every year.

   ____

Name ______________________________ Date ____________

Unit 6 • Vocabulary: Word Families

Fill in the chart below with words that share the base word *use.* Use a dictionary to help you list words. An example for each column has been completed for you.

Prefix + Base Word	Base Word + Suffix	Prefix + Base Word + Suffix
reuse	usable	reusable
______	______	______
______	______	______
______	______	______
______	______	______
______	______	______
______	______	______
______	______	______
______	______	______
______	______	______
______	______	______
______	______	______

Name ______________________________ Date ____________

Unit 6 • Spelling: Sound/Spelling Review

Underline each misspelled word in the following paragraph. Record the word spelled correctly in the space following the paragraph.

Janet and Hannah owpened a noo shop on the corner. They sell toys, fewd, and clothes for pets. Janet and Hannah owne the shop. Dogs, cats, and other pets are allowed to shop with their families. Every time my dog visits the shop, she gets a bown to choo. I let her pick her owne treats. She likes soft treats moste.

1. ______________________
2. ______________________
3. ______________________
4. ______________________
5. ______________________
6. ______________________
7. ______________________
8. ______________________

Name ______________________________ Date ______________

Unit 6 • Grammar and Mechanics: Review of Pronoun-Antecedent Agreement

Underline the pronoun that correctly completes each sentence.

1. Sonny's mother gave (it / him) a book to read.

2. Kari asked (her / their) mother if she could go to the park.

3. The Smiths enjoyed (his / their) vacation this year.

4. Caleb showed Genevieve (his / her) new baseball glove.

5. Sydney's coat fell in the mud and now (it / she) needs to be washed.

6. Suzy was late for (his / her) doctor appointment.

7. From the back seat, Zoe asked "Are (we / they) almost there?"

8. Darryl won't ride (its / his) bike until (it / he) paints (it / him).

Name ______________________________ Date ____________

Unit 6 • Vocabulary: Review: Word Meanings from Context

Read each sentence below. Write a definition for the underlined word. Use context clues to help you.

1. Without her tape measure, the decorator could only get an <u>approximate</u> measurement of the room.

   Definition: ______________________________

2. Although he lives in the city, Barry prefers a more <u>rustic</u> setting. He spends as much time as he can on his family's farm in the country.

   Definition: ______________________________

3. For dinner Sunday, we went to the <u>smorgasbord</u>. My mother likes the variety of foods there, and my teenage brothers like the opportunity to eat as much as they want without having to pay extra.

   Definition: ______________________________

Name ______________________________ Date ____________

Unit 6 • Spelling: Sound/Spelling Review

Circle each properly spelled word and copy it on the space provided.

1. boi

   boy ____________________

2. unknown

   unnown ____________________

3. werd

   word ____________________

4. harber

   harbor ____________________

5. spoil

   spoyl ____________________

6. garden

   gardin ____________________

Name ______________________ Date ____________

Unit 6 • Grammar and Mechanics: Review of Adjectives and Adverbs

In the following sentences, underline each adjective.

1. The loud ring of the telephone interrupted her sound sleep.
2. The fluffy puppy ran across the soft carpet.
3. Hugh chose two cuddly kittens.
4. The flowers in the garden are beautiful.
5. The breeze is chilly.

In the following sentences, underline each adverb.

6. Claire quietly pulled a book off the library shelf.
7. Kirsten arrived early for the highly important meeting.
8. Yesterday we went to the swimming pool.
9. Tia moved the chair upstairs.
10. The new tablecloth was totally ruined.

Name ______________________ Date __________

Unit 6 • Vocabulary: Review of Metaphor and Simile

Write five sentences using metaphors and similes to describe the following story elements.

1. field mouse: ______________________________

____

____

2. buffalo: ______________________________

____

____

3. the meadow: ______________________________

____

____

4. the dried, yellow grass: ______________________________

____

____

5. the crisp, tangy air: ______________________________

____

____

Name ______________________________ Date ______________

Unit 6 • Spelling: Frequently Misspelled Words

Circle the correctly spelled word in each pair. Copy the word in the space provided.

1. anser

   answer ____________________

2. beleve

   believe ____________________

3. Febuary

   February ____________________

4. suppose

   suppoze ____________________

5. siround

   surround ____________________

6. foreign

   forin ____________________